AF731012

Beginning to Understand and Process Grief

A Guided Grief Journal for Teens and Adults

Appropriate for any loss, non-specific

Let's talk real about grief, grief sucks! We often feel nobody understands, not even ourselves, as the emotions around grief can be so complicated.

This journal was created to help others heal by exploring the complexities of grief. Following the death of my husband and then my 18-year-old son, healing and understanding my grief was imperative to survive. After getting my degree and starting a peer grief support program for children, teens, and adults, I learned there was a process to my grief. It stirred up so much for me that I had to start at the beginning and finally heal from it all.

Grief lasts a lifetime, but when I learned how to allow the joy and grief to walk hand in hand, literally intertwined together, experiencing them both at the same time, I knew I was healing. Spending years teaching youth within our nonprofit on healthy ways to understand grief was the most rewarding experience, and I learned so much. I wanted to share what I have learned to help others find some peace and, at some point, feel joy again.

Use this guided journal to sort out your feelings, gain insight into your grief, and look back and see how you have grown. Once we understand what we are feeling, it's a starting point to processing and working through the tangled threads of a life forever changed. Facing the grief is hard, but I do believe you can do it, deserve to heal, and to find who you are now.

Just like grief, there is no timeline to completing your journal. Grief can look different from day to day, which is what makes it so complicated. Be patient with yourself and don't rush grief or your journey to heal. Be sure to offer yourself grace and compassion as you process your grief; grieving is not a straight line. You don't follow stages and then all done. It is messy, and sometimes you have to work through things multiple times to get through it. Remember, you got out of bed today; that is a win! Celebrate your wins, and be proud of every baby step towards healing you take. Give yourself the same love and kindness you'd offer to someone else. You deserve it!

It takes more strength to face your feelings and be willing to work through them than it does to stuff them down and avoid them. You can't run from grief; it will always catch up to you, and usually that looks similar to a volcano erupting in the middle of a "china shop." There is no other way around this mountain of grief but to slowly climb over it.

This guided journal is intended to foster self-discovery and insight, and to help you not only grow around your grief but with your grief in the healthiest way possible.

Grief is messy; it is okay to sit in the mess, but we don't want to stay there.

About the Author

Hello, and welcome to your guided grief journal. My name is Jennifer Loza. I wanted to share a little about me and why I have created this journal. First and foremost, I am a mom. I was blessed with two boys and a proud Aunt. My journey with grief started in January of 2012 when my husband, Ronnie, unexpectedly passed away at 44 years old. I had just turned forty-one, and our boys were only eighteen and nine at the time. My business was only 6 days old, and our lives were completely turned upside down. I had no clue what I was doing or how to help my kids cope with such a huge loss. Attending grief groups was incredibly helpful until it abruptly closed down, leaving us with no support. I then decided to go back to college, get my degree, and open our own non-profit to support families. To my amazement, I graduated with honors with a Bachelor of Science in psychology and a minor in sociology, and our non-profit, Ronnie's House for Hope, was born.

In October of 2020, just four months after turning eighteen, my youngest son, Steven, passed away from Fentanyl poisoning. Nothing can prepare you for this, and it truly brought me to a place I didn't know existed. A kind of darkness and emptiness that I could have never imagined. It was with his loss that I knew I had two choices. My remaining son and niece were going to lose me, too, or I had to find the strength to heal and live. They deserved for me to be here for them, and I knew that, with the many losses our family has endured (brother-in-law, friends, and other family members), they were watching me, looking to my example of how we would survive.

Everything in this guided journal is a culmination of what we do in our grief groups with kids and adults, and years of healing I have done with the incredible counselor Tania, who has walked the journey with me. I discovered that in order to heal from the loss of my beautiful son, I had to heal all parts of me. Trauma from youth through my adult years had to be tackled to get where I needed to be. To understand my grief, I had to cope with regrets, other lost relationships, trauma from dysfunction within the family, and all the things that led me to this place: a mother without her child.

It was not easy and still is a work in progress, as grief shifts and changes. I will say it has been worth the hard work. My hope is you can start your grief journey knowing you are not alone and just maybe there continues to be a purpose to the pain. If I can help anyone find hope or even discover who they are now, then that helps me heal, too. I promise there is a light at the end of the tunnel; it may be a little dimmer, but keep working towards the light.

How Do I Use This Journal

The great thing is, there is no right or wrong way to use it. You can follow each topic in order, or you can look below for the subject that you may be feeling you connect to most on any particular day. Each topic does not need to be completed in one sitting. As things come to mind, go to your journal and write them down. The benefit is that as you discover things about your grief, you are able to put pen to paper and later go back to reflect on things. It is an opportunity for self-discovery and to see how your grief shows up. For days, you have a lot to say, and there are overflow pages in the back of your journal. Each one has a space to put what entry it is for; use as many as you need to get it all out.

Self-discovery is great, but do not hesitate to reach out to a trusted friend, support group, or professional when needed. Support with self-insight can make all the difference. This journal can also be very helpful for providing professional insight into where you are and what you may want support with processing.

Entries

Entry 1 - Memories

It is so common that one of the fears we have after the death of someone we love is that we will forget them, worrying about forgetting all the little things. Will I remember their voice, how it feels to touch their hand, the way they laughed, or how they hugged me? Will I remember all the things we laughed about, things we did together, and how it felt?

This is a real fear, since we know that over time, we can forget things, especially the little details. Sharing stories and talking about these things can help keep memories alive, and, in a way, keep them present in our lives. There is a saying, "we die twice, once when we die, and the second time when they stop saying your name." As long as we have memories and talk about them, a part of them is still present in our lives.

Forgetting can be particularly scary for younger people; we hear this in grief groups a lot. There are many ways to remember our loved ones, but what works for one person may not work for another. Preserving memories and moments can be as simple as journaling and writing them down, creating photo albums, videos, slideshows, or shadow boxes, just to name a few. It depends on the memories and what works for you, but it is important to do.

For this entry, take some time to think of all those little things. The way they rolled their eyes at bad jokes, sayings they had, or the smallest thing that mattered to you. Remember the things that made them so special to you and left a lasting impact. It can help ease the fear if you can write it down and revisit the qualities you loved so much about your person.

This is also an opportunity to talk with friends and family and ask them to share stories about your loved one. They can even write them down, sharing old stories from their school days or time on the job.

This does not need to be completed in one sitting. As you think of things or a memory pops into your mind, revisit this page and add it. Remembering can feel painful, and it is remembering what was. With grief, almost everything is painful at first. You can do this, and someday you will be glad you did.

Memories

Date ____________

MEMORIES I NEVER WANT TO FORGET

BIG ONE OR SMALL ONES,

THEY ALL MATTER

1
2
3
4
5
6
7
8
9
10
11
12
13
14
15
16
17
18
19
20

Entry 2 - Explore Emotions

Part of healing is understanding the complex emotions that come with it, as they can be very complicated depending on your relationship with the person. Emotions are instinctive responses; feelings are your interpretation of that

Grief comes with a wide range of emotions. I can give you a few examples, but know the list is much longer. Guilt, shame, anger, fear, numbness, sadness, loss, confusion, frustration, abandonment, or even love, hope, loneliness, and gratitude. All of these are normal, and many depend on the relationship you had and the circumstances as to how they died.

You can feel multiple emotions at once, or maybe you are concerned because you are feeling nothing and just numb. If we can identify which emotion we are feeling, it helps us ask, "Why am I feeling it?" Where is it really coming from? Please remember, this process takes time; healing does not happen overnight, and it may take a while to identify the different emotions you have. These emotions change as you start to change as you begin to grow around and move with your grief.

Sometimes it can bring us to a place where we have to face more than just our grief to heal, and we find it is necessary to face other traumas or painful experiences. This was a personal experience for me as I was healing from the loss of my son, having to look at how I got to where I was, like an onion, peeling back many layers all the way to childhood, to start to heal. This process was hard, took a long time, but was necessary. When you face death, it can open doors and windows in your heart that you never realized needed repair. This is the opportunity to look in those doors and windows to finally heal.

On this page, start to identify some of the emotions that have come up for you. It is okay to take your time. Identify as many as you can, and as you feel them, write them down. Try not to overthink and write from the heart. For example, it is okay to be mad at them for leaving or feel guilty. There are no right or wrong answers; just be honest with yourself.

Explore Emotions

Date ___________

LET'S IDENTIFY EMOTIONS. ANY EMOTIONS ARE NORMAL WITH GRIEF, SO LIST ALL THAT YOU EXPERIENCE IN YOUR GRIEF JOURNEY.

1 ______________________________
2 ______________________________
3 ______________________________
4 ______________________________
5 ______________________________
6 ______________________________
7 ______________________________
8 ______________________________
9 ______________________________
10 ______________________________
11 ______________________________
12 ______________________________
13 ______________________________
14 ______________________________
15 ______________________________
16 ______________________________
17 ______________________________
18 ______________________________
19 ______________________________
20 ______________________________

Entry 3 - Secondary Loss

It is very common to have secondary losses. What is a secondary loss? I am so glad you asked. A secondary loss is when you lose something or someone after a death. You could lose friends, family, a job, or anything you felt you had prior to the loss. Loss changes you, and sometimes the people in our lives do not know how to support us or react to our grief. This could cause them to pull away and maybe keep their distance out of fear of doing the wrong thing.

One example would be if you had a parent die, leading to that parent's family becoming distant and less prominent in your life. Another would be if one parent dies, and the other parent is not coping well, is no longer actively parenting, and is distant. Everyone copes differently, and it can be very challenging for families to work through this. It could even be a best friend who feels your grief is too large and pulls away. Intentional or not, the absence of these relationships is another loss for you to grieve.

Secondary losses can be devastating and intensify the grief you are already feeling. Families and relationships can change dramatically following a death as everyone is coping, trying to figure out their own grief. Secondary losses have to be grieved too, just in a different way, and this can be incredibly challenging depending on the loss.

It does not have to be a person or a relationship. It could be a job you lost because you needed time away, sports you loved, or even because of your health. Grief can affect so many parts of our lives, all of which, in turn, affect how we grieve and heal. We learn a lot about ourselves as we go through this journey, and about those around us as well.

Can you identify any secondary losses you have had that have complicated your grief? How has it changed your perspectives? Think about whether these losses are permanent or if there's something that can be done in time to restore them. Not all secondary losses can or should be restored; this depends on what was lost, who was affected, and how the loss occurred. What is important here is protecting your mental health and your own grief journey.

Secondary Loss

Date

IDENTIFY SECONDARY LOSSES YOU'VE EXPERIENCED IN YOUR GRIEF JOURNEY. THESE LOSSES DESERVE TO BE ACKNOWLEDGED AND GRIEVED AS WELL.

1
2
3
4
5
6
7
8
9
10
11
12
13
14
15

Notes

Entry 4 - Things you Can't Control

When someone close to us who is a regular part of our lives dies, it creates a void and a change that is out of our control. This tends to trickle down into many parts of our everyday lives, making it hard to manage, as most of us do not like feeling out of control.

This can be an issue in so many parts of our lives; not just the lack of control that they died, but it could change our living situation, our relationships, how we live, and how we see ourselves. It can also affect your health, how people treat you, or how you treat others. Change is inevitable, even without loss; it is a normal part of life, and nothing stays the same forever. It is definitely a reality when someone significant dies. This can be so hard to navigate if you can't identify what you actually have control over, and it can be very helpful to figure out what is realistically within your control and what isn't. The things that are not in your control, it is important to find tools to let go of and focus on what you can do.

This feeling of not having any control over so many things can give us anxiety and stress, making us feel incredibly powerless over our own lives. For some, the feeling is so intense they want to give up, "I can't control anything, so what is the point?" This is a normal part of the grieving process; you are definitely not alone. What can we do to feel as though we have control of anything?

For this page, we want to identify what we can realistically control and what we can't. There is nothing we can do about the fact that our loved one died, or how others react to our grief, except how we react to them; often, that means letting go and focusing on what we can control. Grieving takes a tremendous amount of energy; it is best to use that energy wisely. We can control how we care for ourselves by eating well, getting rest, addressing grief, and doing whatever helps our mental, physical, and emotional well-being throughout this journey.

When we are grieving, we can be overwhelmed with things we can't control. It can be incredibly helpful to acknowledge those things. Part of healing is allowing yourself to heal from what makes no sense at all, and release what is completely out of our hands.

Control

Date ________

ON ONE SIDE, IDENTIFY THINGS OUT OF YOUR CONTROL. ON THE OTHER THINGS THAT ARE.

IN MY CONTROL	OUT OF MY CONTROL

Entry 5 - What is Happening to Me?

Grief affects not only our hearts but also every part of our bodies, literally changing our brains as they begin to process the new reality. Some experiences you may have include stomachaches, body aches, headaches, fatigue, and even grief brain. Grief brain makes it difficult to concentrate, causing forgetfulness, and hinders the ability to put thoughts together. The stress you can feel from grief and unresolved grief can even make you sick, which can lead to chronic illness. You may be feeling changes in your body without even connecting that your grief is a contributor to it.

So what can we do? Some things, like grief brain, take time while your brain processes and adapts to the loss. It takes time for new connections to form in the brain as it adapts to a new reality. This is also the brain's way of protecting itself from experiencing the grief all at once. We can help by writing things down and not overwhelming ourselves as much as possible. Other things we can do are bedtime routines to help us sleep, eating better, and exercising to help with the aches, pains, and restlessness we can feel. I know it sounds easy, but I don’t feel like doing any of this! I get it, this is not meant to be done at once. Grieving and healing are about baby steps; taking each day, hour, or moment at a time.

Only when we identify the issues can we take action to make a change and help ourselves. In this entry, identify things you have noticed that have changed in your body, then come up with at least one thing you can do to improve it. Keep in mind that if we ignore changes, you could be setting yourself up for larger issues than they need to be by addressing them. These kinds of changes can be immediate or even over the course of a year or more. The benefit of writing things down is that it helps us become aware of our minds and bodies over time.

Keep in mind that processing grief and acknowledging it will help ease these symptoms over time. Being proactive can be a big part of your healing.

What is Happening?

Date ________

WHAT SYMPTOMS OF GRIEF ARE YOU FEELING IN YOUR BODY, AND WHAT ONE THING CAN YOU DO.

SYMPTOM	ONE THING I CAN DO

Entry 6 - Who Is My Support System?

It is important to have a support system, big or small, especially as your grief changes and evolves, your support system will too. Grief is uncomfortable for so many people; they do not know how to support a grieving person and can become awkward, maybe even keep a distance from you. You can be surprised by the people who show up to truly support you in ways that are helpful and healthy; you may not expect them to be the ones who were most helpful to you.

Remember, when talking about a support system, it is not the quantity but the quality of the support given that is really important. Some may have the best of intentions, but simply do not know how to support you in the way you need them to. They may want to fix it, tell you how to grieve, want you to feel joy too quickly, give tons of advice, and not allow you to grieve in the way that works for you. It is okay to limit access to those people and to be selective who you share your grief with. Your support system should act as a sanctuary where your truth can be spoken without a filter. They should, however, be able to just sit and listen, meeting you where you are at the moment.

When you think of your support system, you work from the inside out. You have the inner circle where you can feel safe to share everything openly and honestly. Then the next circle out, you can share but maybe not as deeply, and so on. You may have already experienced that everyone in the beginning says they will be there, offer support, and be there if you need them. This is something that happens to almost, if not all, grieving people. Time will show you who your tribe through grief will be.

This entry identifies your current support system. Who has been consistent in showing up? Who is showing up in the most helpful ways? It is okay to limit your circles, especially early on in your grief, to ensure those you are around are truly supporting you in a way that is most helpful to you. Support, like grief, is fluid and will change.

Support System

Date ________

SUPPORT SYSTEMS ARE MORE THAN PEOPLE. IT CAN BE CHURCH GROUPS, GRIEF GROUPS, CLUBS, ANYWHERE YOU GAIN SUPPORT. WRITE THE NAMES OF YOUR SUPPORTS IN THE APPROPRIATE CIRCLES.

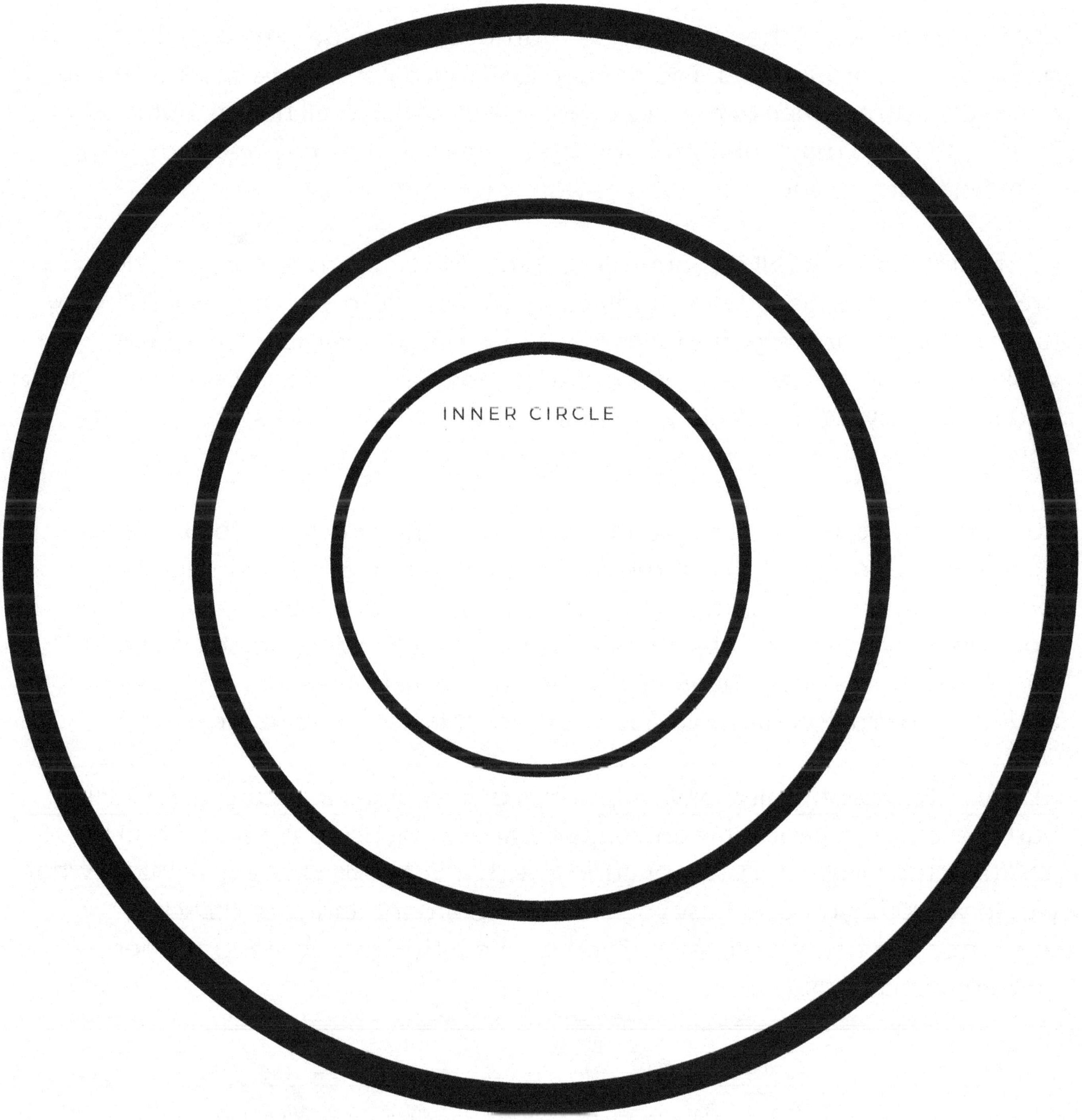

Entry 7 - Self-care, Who Has Time for That?

Self-care is absolutely vital when you are grieving, although it can be difficult to put your care first, you have to make time for it. Taking time for self-care is not only necessary for mental health but also for physical, spiritual, and emotional health. This is important all the time, not just while you are grieving. It does, however, play a vital role in healing.

Everyone has heard the saying about putting your oxygen mask on first, then helping those around you. There is a reason for that, because it is true. It can feel selfish sometimes to prioritize your needs and overall health, but it is not. There can be so many negative consequences if you do not, and that is not beneficial for you and those who rely on you.

Grief can take a big toll on your mind, spirit, and body, so to heal, you need to protect those things as best as you can with what is in your control. Self-care looks different for everyone; for some, it may be exercise, journaling, and long walks. For others (like me), it is building things, DIY projects around the house, and letting my mom get creative in any way possible. Find what works for you.

So right now you may be thinking, I don't have the energy, time, or desire to do anything. You want to put the covers over your head, blocking out the world and reality. That is absolutely valid, and from time to time, okay to do. Again, day by day with baby steps, it is important to offer yourself some love and grace. This is about healing at your own pace, taking small positive steps, and making small achievable goals. It is not meant to create more stress.

In this entry, identify all the ways you can give yourself self-care. Is it music, baths, exercise, a wreck it room, or just walks? Maybe you're an animal lover and take the dogs for a walk, or cuddle with a goat, who knows. Think of what would work for you, and how you would implement it in your daily life, remembering to keep all parts of you in mind: the body, emotions, mental, and physical needs.

Self-Care

Date ________

WHAT CAN YOU DO FOR SELF-CARE? HINT: WHAT WORKS FOR ONE OFTEN WORKS FOR ALL, THAT IS CARE FOR THE WHOLE SELF..

SELF-CARE FOR SPIRIT & BODY	SELF-CARE FOR EMOTIONAL AND MENTAL HEALTH
1	
2	
3	
4	
5	
6	
7	
8	
9	
10	
11	
12	
13	
14	
15	
16	
17	
18	

Entry 8 - Check-In Day.

So what is the point of a check-in day? Some days, you need to vent and get it all out: frustrations, thoughts, anger, or whatever is weighing on you. You know those days you want to get in the car, turn the music up really loud, and just scream at the windshield, telling it everything that has been bottled up inside; we all have those days.

With this guided grief journal, you have prompts to help you focus on one aspect of your grief. Today, simply write, don't really think about what you are writing. Put pen to paper and let it flow with whatever is on your mind. If one page isn't enough, there are extra pages at the back of the journal for overflow.

This can be so cathartic to release all the yuck that can stick to you, like a warm shower after working outside on a hot day, allowing it to fall off you. Maybe you have thoughts you don't want to say out loud or can't, so you can write them down, remembering this is your journal. If you have things you need to say and think to yourself, "If someone ever saw this, what would they think?" Write it down anyway, and when you are done, tear out the page and destroy it. The goal here is to release it, get it out.

Free writing is best when done without distractions, keeping the television off, music off, somewhere it is quiet, and you're alone to just let your mind go, writing down whatever pops into it. Pick a quiet place where you can be left alone for half an hour.

It may not always make sense since you are writing whatever pops into your mind at the moment. You may start writing about one thing and quickly veer off to another, and that is actually perfect! Let it all flow freely and honestly.

You may be very surprised at what comes to mind. You might find that things you didn't even realize were swirling around in there. It is really helpful in refocusing your thoughts and giving you almost a clean slate. It definitely helps to purge those lingering, sometimes intrusive thoughts.

Check-In Day

Date ________

JUST WRITE ANY THOUGHTS THAT YOU HAVE TODAY THAT YOU WANT TO RELEASE. NO THINKING, JUST PEN TO PAPER AND UNFILTERED THOUGHTS.

Entry 9 - Holidays and Special Occasions

How do I cope with holidays, birthdays, and special occasions without them? This is a loaded question and one of the most challenging things every griever has to figure out, especially in the first couple of years. Everything is different now; am I supposed to pretend it is all the same? The anxiety that comes with all the firsts can be so overwhelming, trying to figure out how to do it to make others happy, at the risk of your own comfort or ability. Not wanting to lose traditions, yet nothing feels the same, and it is harder to try to keep them.

The most important thing to remember is that you need to do whatever is best for you and your immediate family. You may receive pressure from family, especially on holidays, to do what you've always done. For some, this may work; for others, you can't even imagine trying to pretend it is the same. On a personal note, our family experienced this. I have no regrets about talking to my children and changing every holiday the first year in a way that worked for us; family members who were not happy got over it. They later understood.

It is okay to keep traditions if that is something you want to do, but it is also great to create new ones. Sometimes you will have family who want to celebrate these days exactly as they were; however, you may not be ready for that. Some people want to gather for birthdays and anniversaries, while others want to be alone. Each holiday or special occasion will feel different. Just as you will feel different with each one. It is so important that you listen to your heart and do what you think you can handle and what feels the most comfortable.

The key to holidays and special occasions is to communicate with your immediate family, see how they are feeling, but also share where you are. No matter what, it will be different; you will feel the absence no matter what you do. The first year is about getting through it. The second year tends to be a little more difficult as the shock and numbness wear off and reality sinks in.

Think of ways you can include them in the holidays and special occasions. Maybe attend a candlelighting, write letters, share memories, or do anything that makes you feel they were included, even in the smallest of ways.

Special Days

Date ________

WHAT ARE SOME WAYS YOU CAN REMEMBER AND INCLUDE YOUR LOVED ONE ON HOLIDAYS AND SPECIAL OCCASIONS?

1	16
2	17
3	18
4	19
5	20
6	21
7	22
8	23
9	24
10	25
11	26
12	27
13	28
14	29
15	30

Entry 10 - Things I Wish Others Understood About My Grief

The unfortunate reality of grief is that most people within your circle probably won't understand it unless they have experienced a similar loss. If you are grieving the loss of a child, someone who has had a husband die will not understand; they are very different losses. This is sort of a tricky thing to navigate for both you and them. They want to be there to support you, trying to say and do all the right things. We, as the grievers, want the support, but it can feel more frustrating because they just don't seem to get it. How could they if they have not experienced it? They can imagine how you feel, but truly understand how they could.

Not only are the types of loss different, but so are the relationships, how you process them, current circumstances, family dynamics, and so much more. Part of prays they would just get it, and the other part is glad they have never experienced it and can't understand.

This also comes into play when you look at your support system. So what do we do if no one around my inner circle has experienced anything similar? It is okay to be honest and tell them about your grief, tell them what you wish they understood, and ask them to simply hold space for you. Not to necessarily try to understand.

A grief support group is also very helpful and worth considering. You are in a group with others to understand who experienced it and to seek healing. They tend to be very open, welcoming, and nonjudgmental. If the group setting is not for you, a grief counselor can be very helpful.

In this entry, think about what you want others to know about your grief. How it shows up in you, how it feels, how you process it, and what you need to feel supported. Put it all out there. It is okay to speak out loud about what it is you need by sharing what your grief looks like.

What others should know

Date ________

WHAT YOU WISH OTHERS UNDERSTOOD ABOUT YOUR GRIEF.

Extra pages in the back if more space is needed

Entry 11 - If I Could Have One More Conversation, I Would Say...

I don't know any griever who has not had the thought of what one more conversation would be like and all they would want to say. It may be because you did not get to say goodbye, maybe you were not on good terms, or it could be that you just have so many things you felt were unsaid. This is a common feeling that we just need to tell them one more time or one more thing.

This can be agonizing if you really feel there are things that you have to say. So if you could have one more conversation, what do you want to say? Rather, what do you need to say to assist you in moving forward? Take your time and give this some thought. You could be grieving a friend with whom you had a falling out the last time you spoke, or a parent with whom you are estranged. This can make healing very difficult, with these unsettled issues that seem impossible to resolve.

Do you need to say goodbye? Do you need to say sorry? Maybe you just need to make sure they know how much you loved them. Although it may sound crazy, talk to them. I was told something once that really stuck with me: "They are not dead, just different." I really thought about that, and it made me more comfortable just sitting down to talk with my husband and my son. If you don't get the things in your head and your heart out, they will swirl around, making you feel stuck in this place like blocks of cement around your ankles. This can go back to what you can and can't control.

If the idea of sitting and just talking is hard, write letters. Writing is an amazing way to clear our thoughts and make room for healing. You can say anything at all. However you choose to release it, the point is to release it. Holding on to the "I should have said, or would have said" only holds you hostage in that place.

For this entry, write out what it is you would like to say or feel you need to say. It will likely take more than one page, so you will find additional pages in the back of the journal. Speak from your heart and let it all release out just like the opening of a dam. Take your time and don't rush it. Please make sure you get it all in there.

One More Talk

Date ________

IF I HAD ONE MORE CONVERSATION,
THIS IS WHAT I WOULD SAY

Extra pages in back if more space is needed

Entry 12 - What am I Most Afraid of

There is so much fear that comes with grief, and what we fear is different for everyone. How do I even begin to move forward without my person? Maybe you're worried about finances or family dynamics? You may be worried about where the relationship was and what you last said. You can worry about the future and how it unfolds, and the list can go on and on. Depending on the loss you've experienced, the things that you fear will be different; someone who is grieving a spouse would have different fears than someone who is grieving a child or parent.

Fear is one of those things that can make moving forward in your grief so incredibly hard; facing fear can be paralyzing and stop you in your tracks. This is one of the emotions that can take hold of your thoughts and your health, essentially holding you hostage. You'd rather put the covers over your head, just stay in bed, and not deal with any of it, and that is totally understandable. You have already had to confront this horrible loss and all the emotions that go with it, and it is difficult to find a path forward. Anytime we face the unknown, sometimes an unknown that we can never have the answer to it can be terrifying.

This entry encourages you to think more deeply about your fears and whether you have any control over them. For example, you're afraid of the changes in family dynamics? There is only so much you can control, and you can't change how others react to loss. Maybe the fear is that they are not okay where they are now, which is hard to resolve since we can't get definitive answers and have to look inward for solace.

If you can begin to identify your fears, you can begin to understand what you can take control of and what you may need to release. Fear is like grief; there is no way around it, you can't go under it or over it. You must go through it. If you don't at some point face it and work through it, it can very much stall your grief process, prolonging the healing process.

Start by identifying everything you are afraid of, the big and small, it doesn't matter. Once you can identify and articulate them, you'll be able to tackle them in baby steps.

What I am Afraid of

Date ________

WRITE DOWN THE THINGS YOU ARE AFRAID OF. FEARS TO PARALYZE YOU, LET'S START BY IDENTIFYING THEM.

1	16
2	17
3	18
4	19
5	20
6	21
7	22
8	23
9	24
10	25
11	26
12	27
13	28
14	29
15	30

Entry 13 - Lessons They Taught Me

When we are grieving, it is easy to focus on the loss since the absence is so profound. We focus on the fact that they are no longer here; it is not fair, we want them back, and all that they will miss. This is normal; we love them, and our lives don't feel whole without them. In other words, GRIEF SUCKS!

I want you to focus on something else for a little bit. With a little distance from the time of loss, it is easier for us to think of all the ways they impacted our lives and what they taught us. What are all the lessons they taught you? Everyone has a different impact on our lives, depending on the role they play.

Take some time to really think about it. What did their character teach you, and what direct lessons did you learn? How has this person being a part of your life impacted your perspective on your own life? Did they hold values in the way they lived life that you could look up to? Maybe they supported you through a difficult time that you really appreciated.

This is where we pause from the pain of loss and focus on the blessings and gifts that will stay with us long after they are gone. These are the things we hold on to with all our might as the years go on, and they are the things we celebrate, pass down to others, and that allow us to smile when we think of them.

On those days when the grief hits you like a tsunami, and you're being taken down with powerful, never-ending waves, these things are like having a life vest. We can hold on to everything they taught us and the gifts they left us to help us not only move forward with them but also do so with gratitude and love.

Allow yourself to think about all the wonderful things you did together, the memories you made, and what you loved about them. Sometimes the smallest thing leaves a lifelong lesson. What are the wonderful gifts you will continue to carry for years to come?

Lessons They Taught Me

Date ________

WHAT LESSONS DID YOU LEARN FROM YOUR LOVED ONE.

1	16
2	17
3	18
4	19
5	20
6	21
7	22
8	23
9	24
10	25
11	26
12	27
13	28
14	29
15	30

Entry 14 - Check-In Day

Today, let's have a check-in day. A break from all the hard work of grieving, processing, and healing to clear your heart and mind, with one catch. You should focus on all the things you feel you are doing well. We can be our own worst enemies and don't often take time to reflect on all the things we are doing well, or the growth we have made.

Grief is incredibly hard work, work you didn't ask for and would love to have disappear so you can feel "normal" again. The tricky thing is, you will never feel the same kind of "normal" again. You will find a new "normal" with time.

How did you get through today? What did you do that worked for you? What do you feel proud of yourself for? How have you grown from starting the grief journey that has been a positive thing for you? Is there something that you are working on that you feel good about? Is there anything you want to do better? This is more of a self-check-in, but really focus on giving yourself credit for all the small positives, celebrating the baby steps forward.

You can also do the free writing we did earlier. If you are more comfortable with no topic, no thinking, just clearing your mind and putting pen to paper.

Maybe you are starting to see links within activities and how they can work together. So much of healing is about seeing how, by identifying topics, you can expand out to find the root of that emotion, but it does take time. In my own experience, it really took 5 years to go back in the past to heal from my grief. It was such a gift to myself to really take the time.

You deserve to heal. Keep up the great work!

For this entry, just check in. Where are you at today?

Check-In Day

Date ________

WHERE ARE YOU AT TODAY?

Extra pages in back if more space is needed

Entry 15 - What Emotions Have Surprised Me

When we look at all the emotions and feelings that grief provokes, we are sometimes really surprised by how wide the range is. Most people do not realize how complicated grief can be and all that it entails.

We can sometimes think that when we are grieving a significant loss, our emotions and feelings are sadness, and when we grieve, we are sad. The reality is, it can go so much deeper than that. Loss can stir emotions that may have been dormant for a long time without you even realizing it.

We can face things like survivor's guilt, general guilt, anger, and some may even feel relief. If you had a loved one die who suffered a long illness or something like Alzheimer's, it is common to feel relief that they are no longer suffering. Not that you don't feel the other things as well, but relief that, in itself, can lead to guilt for feeling it.

Sometimes these emotions that we feel can be uncomfortable. It doesn't feel right, almost making you feel guilty for the feelings. Please know you are normal, and all the feelings are normal. There truly isn't a right or wrong way to feel when you are grieving; you just feel what you feel, then try to process it.

In this entry, investigate the emotions and feelings that have surprised you. Why are they surprising to you? Do you feel okay about having them, or is it something that makes you uncomfortable? Have you shared these emotions with anyone or kept them to yourself?

When it comes to things you may feel uncomfortable about, I encourage you to offer yourself grace. Grief is hard, messy, and uncomfortable. You are doing your best, but remember it is okay to sit in the mess of grief; you just don't want to stay there.

What Surprised Me

Date ________

EMOTIONS THAT HAVE SURPRISED ME

Extra pages in back if more space is needed

Entry 16 - How I Want to Keep Their Memory Alive

It can be incredibly important to find ways to honor your loved one and keep their memory alive; you don't want the world to forget that they were here and that their lives mattered. You want people to remember the way they impacted your life and the lives of others.

For everyone, this looks so different, and how you do it depends on how the person was to you. Some start foundations or non-profits, usually related to how they died, to make a difference. Sometimes it looks like college scholarships or memorial benches in their favorite place. Maybe your family will do yearly memorial races to raise money for their favorite charity.

Maybe you want to keep their memory alive on a much smaller, more intimate, and more personal scale. What is wonderful is that this can be done in so many ways. It can be very therapeutic to do little things in their memory. For example, on my son's birthday and anniversary, I do small acts of kindness in his memory. It always feels so good to see others smile on those days. It can even be just a gathering with friends where you celebrate them, maybe an annual thing for everyone to get together.

What are some ways that you would like to keep your loved one's memory alive? What are some different things you have thought of, or if you haven't given it a lot of thought, now is a great time?

Definitely take your time to think of all the little ways you can do this. It does not have to be big things like foundations; it can be small things. It can help us feel they will not be forgotten, but it can also help us feel closer to them.

It can also be things you do over time, or maybe something specific you do on the holidays, to help you feel like they are there. The options here are endless, allowing you to do many things if you choose to.

Keeping Memories Alive

Date ________

HOW DO YOU WANT TO KEEP THEIR MEMORY ALIVE

1	16
2	17
3	18
4	19
5	20
6	21
7	22
8	23
9	24
10	25
11	26
12	27
13	28
14	29
15	30

Entry 17 - Do You Look for Signs?

This isn't for everyone, but have you ever looked at a butterfly or hummingbird and thought it was your loved one sending you a sign? It can be anything you see that reminds you of them, or even anything that smells like them. You wonder if they sent them your way. Maybe you run into someone who looks just like them, and you feel an odd kinship with this person, almost like you know them.

It is normal for us to look for signs, since some people believe that they send signals to let us know they are around. Is that you? If not, it is okay to skip this page. For many, this is comforting to think they are never far away. Maybe you talked about it in advance with your person, what signs they may send you.

For me, it is squirrels; for my husband, and fire trucks; and for my son, I always see fire trucks when he is on my mind. Once, I ran into a lady who looked just like my grandmother from her hair, skin, and even her eyes. When she hugged me, it took my breath away and had me in tears because I really felt like I hugged my grandma, who has been gone since 1989.

For some people, they have odd things happen around the house, and you swear it is them messing with you, who knows, right? You may not feel comfortable telling other people out of fear that they won't believe you or think you are crazy. You are not, and who cares what someone else thinks, it is more important how it makes you feel.

What does it hurt in the end, especially if it helps you to feel close to them? It doesn't hurt anyone, so maybe open your mind to possibilities, and who knows what you may see.

In this entry, think back to the things that you have seen and what signs bring you comfort; set an intention of what you would like to see, and ask them to send it. There are never guarantees, but these little acts can help you feel a still presence in your life and a very comforting closeness.

Looking for Signs

Date ________

DO YOU LOOK FOR SIGNS?

1
2
3
4
5
6
7
8
9
10
11
12
13
14
15
16
17
18
19
20
21
22
23
24
25
26
27
28
29
30

Entry 18 - How Has Loss Changed My View of Life?

When we face a significant loss, it can change the way we see life, not just life but also relationships. Later, we will talk about how it has changed YOU, but for right now, let's focus on just your perspective of life.

When you face loss, it can change your perspective on people, life, and the world as a whole. For many, it provokes a desire to understand deeper, to take stock of how they live, what they allow in their lives, and maybe of the people around them.

Does the world feel the same to you? How about the people within your village? Even the work you do may not seem so satisfying anymore, and you feel a strong need for change. When we are faced with the death of a loved one, it does cause us to look at our own mortality, and can have us question how we spend our days and whom we spend them with.

This is a normal part of trying to make sense of it all when nothing makes sense anymore. Very little makes sense after a death, and sometimes what we couldn't see before becomes very clear to us now. I know this sounds odd, but sometimes beautiful, life-changing growth can emerge like a flower out of the darkness of death, leading to wonderful things. These are part of the gifts they leave us if we keep our minds open to see them.

In this entry, think about how your perspective may have changed about life. It doesn't necessarily have to be these huge epiphanies, but even subtle things you've noticed. Have you had any big perspective shifts you think you might act on that could change something for you? Are there any flowers that emerged out of your grief?

This is the first step in recognizing changes in yourself, and an important one to see how your view of the world and how you exist in it can change.

My View of Life

Date ________

HOW HAS YOUR PERSPECTIVE OF LIFE CHANGED?

Entry 19 - What I Wish I Had Done Differently

I think most of us wish we had done something different at one time or another in our lives. We are human, and humans are flawed. Were there things in your relationship with your person that you regret or wish you had handled differently? When we are grieving, we may not always handle our grief in the way we wish we would have and may lash out at someone with misdirected anger.

Let me be the first to say, it is okay that you were not perfect in life or in your grief; nobody is as much as some may like to think so. We are all doing the best we can on any given day, often with an abundance of emotions. Relationships are complicated, and grief is even more complicated. This was a difficult process for me personally. While on my grief journey, there were so many things I wish I had done differently; hindsight is 20/20 after all.

I encourage you to offer yourself grace. If you feel you have apologies or amends to make either to the person who died or someone who may have gotten the wrong end of your grief, it is never too late. Regrets are burdens that will get you stuck, making it incredibly difficult to move forward or heal when you are holding onto regrets or should've, could've, would-haves. We can't go back and change what is done, but we can own it, do better, offer any apologies you feel you owe, but more importantly, forgiveness to yourself.

Regret and guilt will be a weight that eventually takes more than just your peace, but your health. Take this opportunity to think about the things that are weighing on you, the things you wish you did better or differently. This is your opportunity to release those burdens for your peace, healing, and emotional well-being.

Keep in mind that if it is an apology to someone living, you cannot control how they will respond, and their willingness to forgive is up to them. The freedom and peace that come from the apology are for you.

Wish I Did Better

Date ________

WHAT I WISH I WOULD HAVE DONE BETTER

Extra pages in back if more space is needed

Entry 20 - Who Am I Now?

Grief changes you; that is inevitable. You'll never be the same person you were before the loss. It changes all parts of your being, mentally, emotionally, physically, and how you now see yourself. It can be quite the challenge to figure out who you are now. There will be those who desperately want you to be your old self again, because to them, that means you are okay. They don't understand that the person died when your person died, and you need time to figure out how that looks, like a toddler learning to walk.

Figuring out who you are now will take time as you work through your grief and the "new" you is created. As you go through this journey, you have to keep in mind that grief never ends; you will grow around it with time, but it does not just go away, just as our love for them never does. It will soften, and you'll learn to adjust to the new reality. You will evolve into who you are now as this happens. You know you are healing when you learn to allow the grief and joy that are intertwined together to walk with you as one. Just because you feel one does not mean you can't feel the other.

Take some time to really think about the person you were before this loss and who you've grown to be now. What do you see differently about your life, yourself, and the relationships you have? In what ways have you grown around your grief? Is there anything that you now do differently? Is there anything that you have learned about yourself in your grief journey that surprised you?

Taking steps to heal, face hard things, and allow yourself to grow takes tremendous courage and bravery. You hear people say to stay strong. Well, it takes far more strength to look grief in the eyes and face it head-on than it does to bury it and try to avoid it. It takes a very strong person to take these steps, sometimes facing things we are not proud of.

So, in this last entry lets explore who you are now. You have done a lot of work, and I hope that you are proud of all your accomplishments, big and small. Grief is hard, and working through it is a gift to yourself that you deserve.

Who am I Now

Date ________

WHO AM I NOW

Extra pages in back if more space is needed

This is only the Beginning

You made it through your guided journal, and I am sure it was not easy. My hope is that you were able to gain some insight into the craziness that runs through our brains and bodies when we are grieving. It is a starting point to take you to the next level of healing and self-awareness.

I went through all these steps myself as I grieved for my two most significant losses: my husband and son. That is why creating something that can help others was so important. My grief is always right there close to me, and I can reach it anytime, but at the same time, with all the grief work I have done, there is a level of peace I have never felt before. I know they would be really proud of taking the worst pain I have ever experienced and choosing to heal and live again. I really hope this will be a starting point for you, too.

Please remember to be kind to yourself. Grief is hard and can be very messy, so we don't always manage it right. The waves of grief will come and go, but there will also be a tide that eventually brings you back to a shore of unexpected strength. Roll with the waves and give yourself love and grace on the days it feels more like a typhoon. I promise it will not feel this way forever. In my opinion, time does not heal all wounds, but it does allow them to scar over, leaving us not so raw.

Keep in mind that people don't mean to say things that hurt; they truly just don't know what to say, so be patient with them and yourself. Remember, it is okay to share how you feel, honor your grief, and how your grief shows up in you. Celebrate the small accomplishments and just keep going.

I hope this process was as helpful for you as you start healing. My hope is you'll be able to expand on all the work you have done and keep striving to find your joy and peace.

Only a Beginning

OVERFLOW
PAGES

TITLE PAGE

OVERFLOW
PAGES

TITLE PAGE

OVERFLOW PAGES

TITLE PAGE

OVERFLOW
PAGES

TITLE PAGE

OVERFLOW
PAGES

TITLE PAGE

OVERFLOW
PAGES

TITLE PAGE

OVERFLOW
PAGES

TITLE PAGE

OVERFLOW PAGES

TITLE PAGE

OVERFLOW PAGES

TITLE PAGE

OVERFLOW
PAGES

TITLE PAGE

OVERFLOW PAGES

TITLE PAGE

OVERFLOW
PAGES

TITLE PAGE

OVERFLOW
PAGES

TITLE PAGE

OVERFLOW
PAGES

TITLE PAGE

OVERFLOW
PAGES

TITLE PAGE

OVERFLOW
PAGES

TITLE PAGE

OVERFLOW
PAGES

TITLE PAGE

OVERFLOW
PAGES

TITLE PAGE

OVERFLOW
PAGES

TITLE PAGE

OVERFLOW PAGES

TITLE PAGE

OVERFLOW
PAGES

TITLE PAGE

OVERFLOW PAGES

TITLE PAGE

OVERFLOW
PAGES

TITLE PAGE

OVERFLOW
PAGES

TITLE PAGE

OVERFLOW
PAGES

TITLE PAGE

ADD YOUR FAVORITE PHOTOS, LETTERS, OR MOMENTOS

ADD YOUR FAVORITE
PHOTOS, LETTERS, OR
MOMENTOS

ADD YOUR FAVORITE
PHOTOS, LETTERS, OR
MOMENTOS

ADD YOUR FAVORITE PHOTOS, LETTERS, OR MOMENTOS

ADD YOUR FAVORITE PHOTOS, LETTERS, OR MOMENTOS

ADD YOUR FAVORITE
PHOTOS, LETTERS, OR
MOMENTOS

ADD YOUR FAVORITE PHOTOS, LETTERS, OR MOMENTOS

Made in the USA
Monee, IL
02 November 2026

67379294R00044